Simple Techniques for Managing Your Finances

MAXIMIZE YOUR INCOME

REDUCE EXPENDITURE

MAKE AN INVESTMENT

Geary Reid

ISBN: 978-976-8305-23-7

Acknowledgements

Great thanks must be expressed to the following people:

The heavenly Father, for granting me the wisdom and inspiration to record the information in this book, which I began on January 2, 2003, and completed on May 15, 2003; my family, for their continued encouragement and support regarding various challenges; and several people who have assisted with reviewing and editing the book:

- Cheryl Noel
- Paula Reid-Hilliman
- Christine Spencer-Coates, BSc. & Dip. in Pub. Mgmt.
- Julius Campbell, BA Christian Education, BSc. Civil Engineering, CAPM
- Hance Theodore, CIA, ACCA
- Terrance Thomas, Diploma in Land Surveying
- Joseph Wangija, Dip. Human Rights and Youth Development, B.A. Adult Education

To you, the reader: have fun while reading, and grasp and practice what you learn so that this world will become a better place. Many people are depending on your guidance. We all need a shoulder to lean on and a hand to guide us.

Geary Reid
MBA, FCCA, FAAPM, MPM, CAT

Reid's Learning Institute and Business Consultancy

reidnlearn.com

Amazon: amazon.com/author/gearyreid

Facebook: Reid n Learn

Instagram: Reid n Learn

LinkedIn: Reid's Learning Institute
and Business Consultancy

199 Kuru - Kururu, Soesdyke Linden Highway
Guyana, South America

Table of Contents

Introduction 1

Part One: Business Ventures 3

   1. Trading 3

   2. Small Business Investment 5

   3. Maximizing Your Potential 7

   4. Marketing and Advertising 9

   5. Plan Big 11

   6. Managing Your Credit 12

   7. Banking 13

   8. Demand for Money 14

   9. Planning Your Finance 16

   10. Hire Purchases 18

Part Two: Family Income 20

   11. 1+1=2 20

   12. Maximizing Your Talent 21

   13. Leave an Investment for Your Children 22

   14. Ageing 23

   15. Family Planning 24

   16. Planning Your Wedding 25

   17. Helping Within the Home 28

   18. Peer Pressure Purchasing 30

   19. School and School Supplies 31

Part Three: Cost Reduction 33

   20. Health and Nutrition 33

21. Farming for Self-Sufficiency 35

22. Preserve Your Valuable Antiques 37

23. Secondhand Purchases 38

24. Repairs and Maintenance 39

25. Electricity and Electrical Appliances 40

26. Reducing Unprofitable Expenses 42

27. Security of Your Property and Possessions 44

28. Dispose of Damaged or Unnecessary Equipment/Items 45

29. Choose Carefully When Purchasing from Individuals 46

30. Use Professionals to Perform Professional Work 47

31. During the Holidays 48

32. Transportation Services 49

33. Household Expenses 51

34. Follow Safety Regulations 53

Reference List 55

About the Author 56

Introduction

Your money is too valuable to be wasted or misused and, therefore, using it wisely will maximize your accomplishments. The changes money management will bring about in your life may have a chain effect on the lives of many other persons and things.

This book puts forward simple ideas as to how you can sensibly manage your finances. It is divided into three main areas: **Business Ventures**, **Family Income** and **Cost Reduction**. Under each heading, several important topics are dealt with to give an all-encompassing look at the subject.

Living your life to its fullest and enjoying every opportunity that comes your way is but one approach to life here on earth. Your ability to manage finances prudently will allow you to reach where many persons have not gone, and make a name for yourself. We all have said or heard others say "if I had more time, I would try to spend wisely" or "I have wasted a lot of money". Many of us have made financial mistakes, but this does not mean we have to continue to mismanage our finances.

Most persons are guilty of overspending. In most cases, they lack basic financial skills. If an individual starts monitoring their finances, whether on a daily, weekly, monthly or yearly basis, they may be alarmed to discover that they normally spend more than they earn. A big question to you is, "Where does this leave you?"

You will explore many simple but useful tips for good financial management in this book. It is hoped that you will follow these simple guidelines and be wiser in your spending.

This book has been an inspiration from God. It was written to help every reader be a master over their own finances. The author was prompted to write this book after he was approached by a friend who asked for this topic to be discussed with members of a group.

People are sometimes unable to find appropriate financial books that relate to their personal financial lives, but this book is intended to reach both believers and non-believers. The non-believers will find the biblical principles discussed in this book relevant in guiding their financial lives.

This book was written to help every individual grasp simple and practical terms. Reading this book will not only equip you with theoretical knowledge, but also allow you to put into practice those things that you have learned and become a better steward of your resources.

Make a change in your life with what you already have.

Part One

Business Ventures

1. Trading

Any individual who is involved in buying and selling can make a healthy profit within a short time or even on a long-term basis. Even though you may be surrounded by several competitors, be confident and carry out your business professionally.

Whatever the product you are trading, avoid placing a very large price on it. Large markups will chase away many customers. Therefore, use a small markup that you can work with. Remember, customers look at quality and price as two main influencing factors when purchasing from a business or person.

When the markup is high, the selling price will be high and fewer customers may purchase from your business. When the price is low, more persons will purchase from your business. Regular small sales may sometimes be better than large but slow sales. Your market share will increase as more persons purchase from the business, and soon, they may become regular customers.

For example, Store X sells Sharp televisions at a markup of $5 for each television set. Store X sells 40 Sharp televisions per week ($5 × 40 = $200).

Store Y sells Sharp televisions at a markup of $8 for each television set. Store Y sells 20 Sharp television per week ($8 × 20 = $160).

From the example shown above, Store X sells twice as many televisions as Store Y and makes $40 more per week than Store Y ($200 − 160 = $40). Soon, Store X may attract more customers from Store Y and the number of televisions sold would be expected to increase in the future.

At the end of the year, Store X would have made a larger profit than Store Y. Store X sells the Sharp televisions for $3 less than Store Y, but makes

$2,080 ($40 × 52 weeks) more per annum than Store Y. If some of Store Y's customers switch and begin to purchase from Store X, then its profit will be even greater.

The guiding principle is that *when the selling price is lower, the demand may be greater as more persons may purchase, therefore the profit will be bigger.* A slight reduction in price may result in a significant increase in demand for your product, resulting in greater total sales.

Always remember to sell a quality product at a reasonable price. Make your customers interested; do not look for large returns on your investment immediately. Good customer relationship built over time is also a factor that strongly affects sales.

Throughout the business operation, maintain a standard of excellence, and soon your business' name will speak for itself. Your business will soon become a household name.

Be aware, however, that a business that is unable to make a reasonable profit could soon be forced out of existence. Therefore, set out to make a penny a day (a small but reasonable profit) rather than a dollar in a year's time, because you may never be able to make the dollar you forecasted.

2. Small Business Investment

If you do not have a sewing machine, you can probably purchase one and practice to sew. After learning some basic skills, you may be able to sew curtains, drapes, pillowcases, kitchen towels, bedsheets, aprons, etc. As you learn more, you can then sew clothes for yourself. Improve your skills, if necessary, by attending classes. Later, you can design and make items to sell to the public. You will be maximizing the use of your time and earning additional dollars.

Purchase a gas stove. Bake for the family – bread, cakes, pastries, etc. These small items can go into your lunch container or your children's lunch kits. Once you have developed those skills, begin baking wedding cakes, cakes with icing, and pastries for shops or schoolchildren. What are you waiting for?

If you purchase a refrigerator or freezer, then make ice cream, fruit punch or fruit juice to sell, but remember that quality is important.

The revenue from these activities can possibly pay your electricity bill and pay for the refrigerator or freezer if it was bought on a hire purchase agreement. Alternatively, you may wish to use the extra cash to purchase your children's school clothes and supplies, or fulfill other incurred or essential bills.

Invest in a simple grass cutting (land mower) machine that can provide service for both the public and you. Make your bodybuilding exercise equipment available to the public at a reasonable fee. Practice fixing something that has been damaged and soon you will recognize that you have developed a skill.

Purchase literature (books) and devour them to increase your knowledge and then apply it to develop a skill. Share your knowledge with your family, friends and neighbors. Soon, others will know of your knowledge and they may request your service and expertise, for a fee.

Use the space below your home to do some business. The extra space in your yard can also be used to do something that you know best. If suitable, you can even rent out the extra space in your house. For example, you can convert an empty yard into a public parking lot.

3. Maximizing Your Potential

God has blessed you with talents that can have an impact on the nation. You must maximize the use of them. As Proverbs 18:16 says, "A man's gift *maketh* room for him, and bringeth him before great men." Whatever the gift God has blessed you with, its effect depends upon you. You are never too small, young, old or inferior to make an impact on the people surrounding you or the nation. Your status and self-esteem will change when you recognize who you are.

When the use of your talent is maximized, your income will also be maximized. Your performance will help to determine your success and income.

In addition to their day job, qualified teachers can utilize their skills and knowledge by teaching evening classes. This extra activity will add income to their home. The family member who cooks delicious meals can offer a service to the public at a reasonable price. Why should housewives sit at home going through the routine (washing, cooking, cleaning, etc.) for years? You can earn some income for the family if you are utilizing your skills to engage in activities that will allow funds to flow to you. Every day must count as an important day for you.

If you have a piece of land that is not being used, then invest in it. You can use it to start your own business or rent it out.

A family member at home can start a "kitchen garden". Once the garden produces food, you will not have to purchase everything for the family from the grocery store. This would reduce some of your household expenditure, and you may soon have more than you can consume, which would then allow you to sell the extra produce to earn additional money.

If you are an excellent reader, why not establish a reading club facility for the public? If you are a good driver, then you can work towards being certified to train other persons to drive, for a fee. A good typist can type documents for the public on his or her own computer.

A family member who is not earning but has available time can possibly start his or her own business or grocery shop. This way, your free time will be converted into business time that will yield an income, to help the family and allow goals to be realized. As the business grows, it can even provide employment for other family members or individuals of the public.

Remember, there is always something that you can do and, when given the chance to do it, give it your best. For Christmas, sew your own curtains, make decorations, do florals, etc. Baking your own special cakes and sharing them with others before any actual selling occurs is a great way to advertise your talent. This is direct and firsthand advertising.

4. Marketing and Advertising

Whatever skills you may possess, if you keep them hidden, no one will know about them. After you have spent several months or years developing your skill or knowledge, make your presence known to those who are unaware of your ability, expertise, product, etc. Whenever you advertise what you possess, you may gain the attention of many.

Remember, you may start small, but the results can lead to so much more. Do not settle for less. Therefore, set targets and work towards them so that they are materialized within the allocated time.

When advertising your skill or knowledge, choose a promotional mix, that will give the best return at a reasonable cost. Ensure that your advertising method influences your target group. If you have an additional product available, which is of good quality, then let the public know about it. For example, Internet cafés also advertise that typing may be done within the same building.

Advertising and marketing must not be viewed as a costly exercise, but an investment that will yield great results if properly and effectively executed.

Research as much as you can before you offer a product or service to others and ensure that every area is properly analyzed. By researching, you should be able to create a product that meets the needs of others.

In selecting your advertising medium, it ought to be cost-effective and able to reach your target market. The forms of media to consider are newspapers, stickers, calendars, magazines, etc. Printed media are long lasting, cost-effective and do not have to be paid for regularly. The use of Internet marketing and social media must be carefully considered, based on the target group.

Ensure that your product is branded and properly labeled, and that the trademark is distinctive. Seek to upgrade your product or service regularly.

Remember, there may be competitors, but do not be intimidated. Some of the competitors might have been there before you and some might have started recently, but you must encourage yourself and be confident about what you can offer to the public. Create a great demand for your product by producing high quality consistently.

5. Plan Big

Although we cannot see into the future, we should be planning big for it. Planning big allows you to confront the present situation with something in mind, rather than being empty-handed.

A small income cannot build a house in a day, but if you save or purchase materials piece by piece, then the goal will eventually be realized. On the other hand, a person who does not plan well for their future will be in great danger. That person will hardly reach any target because no target was set.

You should plan to acquire your own home and at least one vehicle. In addition, do not expect things to be dropping from the sky. Do not expect that God will cause someone to give you their vehicle.

Believers, you serve a big God who will do big things, if you only believe and plan.

Planning is ineffective if it is not properly executed. Every plan must be properly executed so that a rewarding result will be achieved.

Drawing a plan for your house will not bring the house to you, but the plan will often force you to make things happen. A student who wants to be successful and perhaps top the country or school must plan to use the same amount of time available to everyone effectively and efficiently.

Planning is the starting point that will bring great things into your house or life, so plan big and execute the plan. Planning big will give you your own house and allow some extraordinary needs to be met – achievements that may be impossible for some others, will become possible for you.

If you were to build a small house now, what will you do when your family increases in number or relatives visit?

6. Managing Your Credit

Credit is good, but if not properly managed, it will make you many enemies. People who receive credit may sometimes find it difficult to meet their vows or commitments. This may not be because they do not want to honour their vows, but because of changing factors or situations.

Placing the slogan below in your business is not enough. It needs to be reinforced or told to some individuals. Say *"No credit"* when you need to.

Credit Makes Enemies!
We are sorry to announce the death of Mr. Trust.
He was murdered by a Bad Paymaster,
So let us be friends and deal with his brother —
Mr. Cash

The sad part is that some friends may not be able to shop at your business because they rely on credit sales, but the good news is you will soon be making new friends who will help your business grow. The new customers will support you with their cash purchases and soon help to market your business.

Whenever credit operates within a business, your *stock* will be reduced without getting any cash in return. If you are unable to replenish it, then both old and new customers may be lost. New and old customers may seek another business that does not frequently run out of stock, especially since your business may not be as large as the giant/chain stores.

Credit takes cash from the business in the form of stock. Some businesses offer credit, but for a specified period, e.g., seven (7) to thirty-one (31) days.

7. Banking

Banking is important to every individual. You can better monitor your spending if you process most of your financial transactions through the bank or a system that allows you to account for every cent received or issued. With banking, the money is in a safe storehouse, so *your heart need not be troubled.*

Banks often use the deposits of customers to provide funds to other customers who would like to borrow money. Most times, the intended borrower must provide some collateral (securities). The bank may ask the intended borrower to have a savings account with the bank. The advantage of having a savings account is that it gains the customer interest at the same time.

Additionally, having to physically visit the bank to withdraw funds may deter you from making regular withdrawals, which may indirectly cause you to reduce unnecessary spending. Banking also prevents burglars from visiting your home since the money is not stored under your pillow.

Before opting for a fixed deposit, you should consider the terms and conditions for such accounts, including the fact that it may be difficult to withdraw funds in the event of an emergency. If this is a concern for you, then there may be a need to have a savings account instead, which will allow access to your finances at any time.

Fixed deposits should be placed only for the excess funds in your savings account or if you want to gain some interest for the available funds, assuming said funds do not have any intended use in the near future. Fixed deposit terms should be carefully studied first, to avoid committing your finances for a longer period than may be suitable for your operation.

Efforts must be made to increase your savings as the year progresses. Once the savings account attracts interest, then you are expected to receive more funds at the end of the period.

8. Demand for Money

Money is important, and there is always a demand for it. People hold on to money for different reasons.

Based on the Keynesian economics theory (CAT Interactive Text, Level C, Paper 5, 1998), here are reasons people hold on to their savings as money in liquid form rather than investing it:

Transactions Motive

Daily expenses such as transportation, food and newspapers need daily attention and cannot be put off for another day. These expenses do not know the word "wait" and need immediate attention as they arise. For this reason, individuals will hold part of their income.

You are advised to act wisely in these situations, as too much money can be spent due to the transactions motive. Imagine you have spent all of your money in hand – how would you deal with your daily expenses for the rest of the month? Would you walk to work, live without groceries, or unable to purchase diapers and milk for the baby?

Remember, you should try to spend from your earnings, not from expected income.

Precautionary Motive

What happens if cooking gas or gasoline prices go up far above your expectation or a member of your family becomes sick? Without any funds, what would happen in that situation?

Money should be kept for an unexpected event. Individuals ought to leave room in life for the unexpected and be ready to cope with it or at least cushion its effect.

Life is not fixed in the sense that everything remains the same way or operates according to your plans. People, therefore, need to take precautions. On many occasions, sickness does not provide advance notice. Therefore, it could suddenly come upon you, and if you are caught unprepared, your health can be severely endangered, and your family's well-being threatened.

In cases where the breadwinner suddenly becomes sick and is unable to earn an income, what would happen to him or her and the family? Always keep a reserve for the unexpected; you may not have a friend or a financial institution to come to your rescue in critical moments.

Speculative Motive

During the year, some things may sell at a relatively reasonable price or for much less than the average price. It is important to capitalize on those bargains sometimes. Bargains happen at different intervals, but you must be prepared to capitalize on them when the opportunities arise.

For example, in the months of September to November, Christmas items may be sold at an average price, but closer to Christmas, the price suddenly finds wings and takes an upward flight. Do not always believe that "you can fly and touch the sky" in order to reach that new price for the same item.

It may be better to shop for some items that relate to an occasion or festival in advance before the price becomes unreasonable. If your prediction comes to pass, then you will save money because of sensible spending, i.e., planning and executing your spending ahead of the required time.

After certain holiday seasons, some items that can be used for next time around will be sold at very low prices, e.g., decorations, curtains, etc. Likewise, items that are specific to a season may be sold at relatively low prices once the season is over, and you can make good use of those bargains if you have the funds and need the items.

The speculative motive for spending is like using a pair of binoculars or a telescope to see further than your natural eyes can behold.

9. Planning Your Finance

You may feel that the money you work for is never enough to satisfy your needs and wants. However, did you know that the little that you have could take you very far? When managed well, you can do better than those who earn more than you.

When you worked for your earnings, you tend to cherish them well. If you are fortunate to have others freely giving to you, accept it, but manage what you receive wisely also.

Set goals and make a plan showing the steps that you will take in order to achieve those goals. Each goal may require different steps, so in your plan, state the required steps and carefully follow them during execution. Your plans ought to be converted into a budget or included in your budget. Your monthly expenditure ought not to exceed your real *disposable income*.

Budgeting

A budget is a financial plan for a period and needs to be reviewed from time to time against actual expenditure and circumstantial changes. It is not a continuous financial statement. After reviewing your budget against actual performance, you may be surprised to find that some areas of expenditure can be reduced.

Budgeting is not a time-wasting exercise, but a great financial plan for the future. Your performance can only be measured when a budget or target is set. It is often good to compare your actual performance with the budget at various intervals, so that adjustments can be made when the need arises.

Income and Expenditure

Record your income and expenditure. Be smart; prepare your own financial statement, which is an account of your income and expenditure for a period. Use dates when recording your transactions, which will allow you to have a history of income and expenditure for any given period.

When you start to account for your finance, you will be more considerate about your spending, and you may also try to earn more. Such an approach does not make you a cheap person, but a person who considers *value for money*.

Treasures in the hands of fools are like the wind that blows from the East to the West at 100 MPH, which goes swiftly but never returns.

10. Hire Purchases

Hire purchase arrangements must be carefully investigated before committing to them. Once you have made a commitment, it remains yours until the contract is over. Many times, the hire purchase agreement may have some fine print that you did not take the time to read, since you were more interested in having the item.

If you were to acquire an item with zero deposit or down payment, there may be large repayments or high interest involved. This means that, by the end of the period, you may have paid one and a half times or twice the original price of that item.

When purchasing any item on a hire purchase arrangement, especially if it is a mechanical or electrical item, a warranty should be part of your consideration. Look for the same item at different hire purchase stores, compare the offers and try to obtain the best possible offer, which should include a warranty.

Find out what method of calculation is used by the store if possible. When the repayment period at one store is longer than at other stores, be wary that you may be paying much more in the long run. Whatever the hire purchase agreement is, you must be in a comfortable position to pay for the item on a regular basis and you should not have to pay twice for the same item.

For example, compare two different hire purchase agreements for the same item below:

Store A	Store B
Cash price: $100,000	Cash price: $100,000
Initial price if one wants the item on hire purchase: $125,000	Initial price if one wants the item on hire purchase: $120,000

Deposit: $0	Deposit: $12,000
Monthly repayment: $8,000	Monthly repayment: $9,500
Repayment period: 24 months	Repayment period: 18 months
Total paid at the end of the period: $192,000	Total paid at the end of the period: $182,000

(Developed by the author for this literature)

Some stores calculate their cash price by adding a percentage of markup on top of the original cost of the item, then add a percentage of interest to the cash price to determine the hire purchase price.

For example, $100,0000 × 15% (markup) = $15,000.00. The cash price will be $115,000. Then another percentage is added onto the cash price to produce the hire purchase price: $115,000 × 10% = $11,500. Therefore, the final calculated price, i.e., $115,000 + $11,500 = $126,500, will be the total amount to repay.

Other stores calculate their markup percentage from the cash price to derive the hire purchase price and then divide it by the number of months to arrive at the monthly repayment figure.

Some stores request higher deposits or down payments but take small repayment sums.

Part Two
Family Income

11. 1+1=2

For Husband and Wife

Much more can be done when two persons combine their income. Family earnings should be treated as one and not separate. When income is pooled, expenses can also be pooled. This gives a true reflection of what the family's expenditures are, and how the combined income can best cover the expenditures and still have money remaining to satisfy other needs or be saved.

If one member of the family chooses to build the family's house all by themselves, one may take several years and also face considerable financial difficulties, considering the rising rate of inflation. When two streams of income are combined as one, the family unit is seen as one and not divided. *A house that is divided cannot stand.*

If another member of the family starts working, that income is part of the family's income and cannot belong to that individual alone. Many goals will be accomplished with this approach and the family will grow stronger. As the family becomes one, no one individual will be under more strain than another member of the family unit.

12. Maximizing Your Talent

It is easy to give the excuse that you are a physically challenged person and unable to do something. Nevertheless, if you have hands, but no legs, you can still write. Even if you have to move around in a wheelchair, you can braid hair, do manicures, cook, etc. There is so much that you can write or do with your hands that many others may not be able to do. Use your hands, they are blessed by God.

Where there are feet, but no hands, you too are blessed and valuable. Be thankful for life, for you can still walk and talk. What about teaching? What about being an athlete? Your feet can take you further than those who only have hands.

Where there are eyes, but no speech, you can see although you are unable to speak. You can read, type, draw, design, cook or paint. So, use those blessed eyes and see.

Can you sing? Then sing and set new records! Your mouth can do so much more than those who have eyes alone.

Remember that there is no second you, and no one can do things the way you do them. Every individual has different gifts/skills within, and many would wish that they were you. If this is so, then use the very skills that others long so much for.

13. Leave an Investment for Your Children

Proverbs 13:22 says that "A good man leaveth an inheritance to his children's children". If you faced great difficulty as a child, you must try not to pass such struggles on to your children. You ought to be smart enough to break the cycle and make a change.

If there needs to be a change, then let the change begin with you.

Your children and grandchildren will always have good words to mention of their parents or grandparents when they are left with an inheritance. With it, they can go through life with less stress than you might have experienced.

For example, if you were to put some money into a bank account for each child, approximately $1,000 per month from birth, by the time the child reaches the age of 18 and starts working, he or she would have accumulated $216,000. In fact, the amount would probably be larger as interest is added onto the savings over the years.

This form of investment will take your child or children a great way into the future. This money can be used to pay for college or university with no one feeling the expense in a direct or drastic way.

If many parents had adopted this principle, their children might not have died before them *from stress, a nervous breakdown, hypertension, etc.*

14. Ageing

You will need to have a good financial bed before you reach 60–70 years old if you want to be comfortable as you watch your grandchildren and great-grandchildren grow up. It is embarrassing to be heavily dependent on one's children, grandchildren, great-grandchildren, relatives or friends for financial support.

Parents, please leave your young people alone and allow them to live with breathing space. They may be *able to help you for some months or years, but they cannot help you* forever.

Even if you only decide to save at least $1,000 per month when you are 50 years old, you will benefit from an annual saving of $12,000 for the next 10 years until you reach the retirement age of 60, at which point you would have saved $120,000. Whether you are eligible or ineligible for a pension, this sum of money will help in some way.

In addition, the amount in your savings will be higher than what you put in because of interest and, not to forget, you may choose to increase the monthly contributed amount as time progresses. You can also add to this account when you receive a financial blessing, bonus, back pay, promotion, remittance, etc.

Such preparation is like a person who purchases an umbrella in the summer because he or she expects rain to occur sometime in the future. There are some things that you cannot avoid, but if you are prepared for it, you will have a peaceful rest even amidst a storm.

When you cultivate the land, do you eat or sell all the produce? If all is consumed, what will you use to start the process again? Remember that you are not getting younger but rather older.

Many persons have invested in a pension scheme and have the benefit of receiving monthly payments from that scheme.

15. Family Planning

Family planning is a very important factor that cannot be ignored or sidetracked. Every child's demand is different and may even be greater than the previous one, thus your income should be sensibly considered before spending.

When your child or children come along, you must restrain yourself from acquiring many things for the family, or your financial freedom may suddenly vanish. Because of insufficient income, the strength of many families has departed, and marriages are marred with pain, hurt and regrets.

Remember, because prices don't get lower as the years progress, expenses may rise very high, affected by inflation and other economic factors. Therefore, try the best you can to plan your family life well. Family planning will allow you to see your children properly educated, purchase a vehicle, build your house and devote time to God, the family and social activities.

Many times, when family planning is not properly administered, expenses send family members out of their homes seeking any available means of income. However, the child who needs milk cannot wait until all the expenses are cleared or the parents' remuneration increases.

Family planning provides opportunities for family needs to be properly met and saves the children from embarrassment in the future, e.g., it is quite embarrassing to hear parents arrested because they were caught shoplifting items to satisfy a need in their family.

16. Planning Your Wedding

Because your wedding is considered a onetime opportunity that is expected to last until death, you should plan it properly. Weddings should not be treated as dreams that happen in the night and unfold in the morning without guidance. When the earth was formed, the Creator himself took time to place everything on it in order.

Planning will cause you to work hard at present to see the desired future come true. Planning helps motivate an individual and indicates the proper directions to follow.

It is important to consider where you are going to live after your wedding. If both partners do not have a vehicle and one spouse were to follow the other to a new location, consideration must be put into what kind of transportation is available at the new place.

Are you a landholder? When will both of you start to build or occupy the land? All these factors and more are vital to be considered before getting married. If they are not dealt with in advance, they will have a severe effect on the marriage.

These are some questions that you can consider when planning the wedding:

- At which religious organization will the wedding ceremony be held?
- Who will be the officiant of the wedding ceremony?
- Who will be the presenter of the bride?
- Who will be the maid/matron of honor and the bridesmaids?
- Who will be the best man and groomsmen?
- What is the budget for the total cost of the wedding?
- Who and how many people will be invited to the wedding and reception?
- Which reception hall will be used, and how much will it cost?
- What will the program for the ceremony and reception be like?

- What will be the type and size of the cake?
- Who will bake the cake and transport it to the reception hall?
- How many cars will be used in the procession?
- What will be your household needs after the wedding celebration?
- Will you have food in the house after the wedding to start a life together or will you survive on the wedding cake?
- What will be the musical arrangements and their costs?
- What beverages will be served at the reception (fruit juices, canned drinks, etc.), and what is the cost?
- Who will you used for a photographer, and what is the cost?
- Will you pay someone to record the wedding procession?
- What will be the style and cost of the bride's dress?
- What will be the style and cost of the bridegroom's suit?

Remember that these questions are aligned with the cost factors of the wedding and, therefore, some other important information is not mentioned in this chapter.

When the wedding is properly planned, the cost will be known in advance to prevent last-minute frustrations. Because you are aware of the cost in advance, you will make better financial arrangements.

If you are unable to finance all the cost, *you can reduce some areas of expenditure and still have an enjoyable wedding.* It is better to have the wedding at a cost that you can afford, rather than embarrass yourself after the wedding, which can eventually affect your future.

It is very easy to spend more than you have for the wedding by borrowing, but after the great jubilation, you will be faced with the debt. Remember that your income may remain the same after the wedding. This income will be required to satisfy all the expenses incurred.

If friends, family or members of any group that you are associated with want to volunteer their labor, products or services, accept them, especially if you feel comfortable with their offer.

If you make the wedding larger than you can afford, you may probably spoil that once-in-a-lifetime opportunity. A large enough quantity of a particular food or beverage is enough to satisfy most, if not all, guests, so there is no need to provide several different dishes or types of beverages.

Do not allow others to help you plan a bigger wedding than you would like to have. Bear in mind also that you cannot invite the entire world to your wedding, therefore, be very selective as to who you will invite.

When catering for the wedding, leave room for unforeseen expenditures and rising prices for the wedding items. Non-perishable and essential items can be purchased in advance if the need arises, especially if there is some assumption that the price for certain items will increase during the time of the preparation of your wedding.

Manage the cost of the wedding wisely, since you will not want to have expenditures *larger than the honeymoon room.*

In addition to the information shared above, you may not be able to attend every wedding you're invited to, so say no to some invitations. If you are popular, many people will want you to attend their wedding. However, remember that some of the times, you will have to be responsible for *all* the expenses related to attending a wedding that you are invited to.

17. Helping Within the Home

Man/Husband

In many religions and societies, the male is the main authority figure in the home who is expected to lead by example. Do not leave all the work or decisions to the wife; help her. *After all, two hands are always better than one.*

Fathers, whatever you do in the home is beneficial to the family and not just a particular individual, so be willing to help your family. Sometimes the frustration and confusion that wives (or mothers) go through can be eased when husbands decide to help and use their muscles in the home.

You don't have to pay a maid to work in your home if "Mr. Man" decides to bless the family with his time and energy. Among other things, husbands can be involved in the maintenance of the house, cooking, washing clothes, babysitting, maintaining the yard, etc.

Reduce overtime work if you are an employee. Sometimes, the gains from working overtime cannot compensate for the expenses incurred by the family due to your absence. Spend time with the family and see the family grow. Time, energy and money spent on your family are a great investment that will not decay.

Husband, rise early in the morning, have your family devotional time together, and help the wife around the house or kitchen. The work will be done faster, allowing both of you to reach your place of employment on time.

If you have a vehicle and you and your wife are headed in the same direction, then you can minimize transportation expenditure by leaving for work together. Your children may also tag along in the family vehicle to attend school if convenient.

Woman/Wife

If you are not participating in activities in your home, then you may frustrate the family, especially if you are physically capable of offering such assistance. *Is the family constantly purchasing food because persons in the house are unable to cook properly?*

Do not affect your child's health by giving them things that have little or no nutrients. Sometimes, those products that have little or no nutrients may be less costly, but it can result in long-term health expenses for the family that may not be reversible.

Regular washing of small portions of clothes will increase your electricity bill. Consider handwashing when you have to was small portions of clothes, so as to reduce your electricity bill. Bear in mind, however, that dirty clothes should not be washed too infrequently, as leaving them unwashed for prolonged periods can result in them becoming damaged or permanently stained.

If you are not a full-time employee, you may not need a maid for some household activities, especially if husband and wife cooperate and organize their activities. If possible, set up a kitchen garden and reap the produce that will become available from the garden.

Children

Children, obey your parents, do the right thing and live a good life.

Parents, your children can be useful within the home, if you will teach them early and guide them to do certain things properly. Children who learn to be helpful within the home may contribute to a better family life.

Whenever adequate work is allocated to your children, they may not have too much time to be engaged in things that are harmful to society. They can be a source of great help, becoming responsible in the process, and also help to reduce some of the household's expenditure.

A child who grows up with a sense of responsibility will be a good steward of his or her possessions. As a result, you may not have to repeat purchasing the same items for the same child, since that child will take responsibility for whatever is given to him or her, a quality that may even translate to being caring towards others.

Prevent your children from playing around breakable items, e.g., playing cricket near glass windows. Do not allow your children to play games in the house that should be played on a field, since dishes, televisions and other items can be easily broken. Bear in mind that you are not trying to add cost, but rather to get the maximum out of all purchases.

18. Peer Pressure Purchasing

Peer pressure purchasing often happens when you try to match up with your friends, family, society, etc. This kind of purchasing is dangerous, and many times causes an individual to purchase items that they do not need.

Peer pressure purchasing often causes the individual to spend without consulting their budget or sticking to their plans. If your peers influence you, then you can land yourself in severe financial problems. This kind of spending makes the individual spend beyond their means.

If you were born as a twin, your whole life does not have to be spent living in the same pattern as your twin sibling. You need to be yourself and operate as an individual. Do not allow the group to pull you up the mountain when you are not prepared for the climb.

Your projection and plan will be different from many others. Therefore, stick to your plan and watch it materialize. Prevent other from "taking" money out of your pocket. Your pocket is in your possession and you must be in *total control* of it. Many persons tend to buy things that are not on their shopping list because of the influence of a family member, friend or workmate. AVOID THE INFLUENCE OF OTHERS TO SPEND UNNECESSARILY.

19. School and School Supplies

Shop for your children the things that they need. As the parent or guardian, you may be required to pay all the expenses that children incur. Children have more wants than you are able to satisfy. Will you allow them to hurt you financially so as to satisfy their wants?

Give your children the *best things they need.* Do not deny them the opportunity to be educated. Education is expensive, but the reward will always be greater. You are to make a worthy investment into the lives of your children during the time when they are under your direct guidance and support.

Select a school that will give to your child/children the best service. Avoid choosing a school that is far away from your home if there are schools in your community that offer quality education and extracurricular activities that will foster the growth and development of your children.

Children who have to travel very far from home may have to wake up early and retire to bed late, which will have a negative impact on them. Children who have to travel far distances daily may become tired and struggle to concentrate during school sessions. Therefore, while you are expecting great results, they may disappoint you with their inability to produce the desired results.

However, some children have managed long traveling distance and have produced outstanding results. Each parent must assess the situation for their children to make decisions that will help with their development. The cost incurred for schooling ought to produce good results.

As they grow older, some children may want to dress in the *latest style or fashion,* but parents, you will have to monitor them and try to ensure that they make good use of the schooling opportunities, rather than busy themselves with impressing others at your expense.

Purchase quality materials for your children and not several cheap or inexpensive things, which will cost more in the long run. Provide enough clothing so that the children will have enough change of garments as the need arises. When the same few garments are used repeatedly, the material becomes worn and may become a poor reflection of you as a parent.

Preserve important literature that your children possess as it can be used to help others in future. As you may recall, some books you used are still being used by your children and to purchase those books again may be very expensive. Similarly, some of the books used by your children can be passed down to their younger siblings or other children studying the same literature, hence reducing cost.

Part Three
Cost Reduction

20. Health and Nutrition

Your health must be on your priority list, for a healthy body gives healthy results. *You are what you eat.* Reduce the food that harms you and start shopping and eating healthy.

Read the labels before you use the contents. Remember, if you eat poorly, then the doctor's bills will be high. *Good nutrition will reduce your doctor's bill.* Eating well may result in you living much longer.

Some of the problems people suffer from as they advance in age could have been prevented, had they taken the necessary precautions regarding the food they consumed. What you eat will result in either increased medical expenses or living a stronger, longer and healthier life that will give you the blessed opportunity to see many generations to come.

Quantity eating can never replace quality eating. Wherever possible, minimize or reduce the consumption of food grown from fertilizer (inorganic manure). You must be careful with the foods that are available free or at greatly discounted prices, as they may negative effect on your health.

When foodstuff such as fruits and vegetables are in excess on the market, you should maximize the opportunity to consume more vegetables and make your own fruit juices instead of having canned drinks.

Eating well will cause the body to fight some diseases and illnesses, and repair itself without you noticing it or adding an unaffordable bill from the doctor. *What you put in is what you get out. You cannot live long when you eat wrong!*

Ensure that the body is given enough rest and do not overwork it. An overworked body does more harm than good. Exercise is useful for every individual who wants to keep the body fit and healthy and extend their days.

Exercise should be simple, continuous and easy to carry out within the time specified.

Simple activities can lead to a healthy life and body weight:

- Walk on a regular basis. You can increase your distance gradually.
- Consume a balanced diet.
- Use some time to prepare kitchen or flower gardens.
- Take your child or children out for regular walks.
- Engage in family outdoor sports.
- Start daily activities early in the morning.
- Convert leisure time into productive time.
- Avoid excessive sleeping and rest.
- Work diligently and walk briskly.
- Be more involved in physical activities.
- Consume more water and work during the warmth of the day.
- Confine eating only to breakfast, lunch and dinner (avoid eating between these periods).
- Play some music and dance.
- Help your neighbors, friends and families with physical activities, but avoid eating out of your schedule.
- Avoid eating fatty and high-carbohydrate foods.
- Eat healthy and not heavy meals.
- Eat fruits and vegetables as snacks (if necessary).
- Replace some meals with light snacks or fruits.
- Avoid eating too late in the evening.
- Go to the market and purchase your groceries without asking others to do the same for you, if you have the time to do so.

21. Farming for Self-Sufficiency

Crops

Those who sow will reap. When we sow, we can enjoy a harvest. Cultivating the land is a very good thing as it gives you an opportunity to provide something for people to consume. The land is not only a place for individuals to live on but an investment that can yield good results.

Sowing will teach you patience. How? There is a time to sow and a time to reap. If you are diligent in sowing big, the harvest in due time can be large. From the produce you harvest, some can be sold and a portion used by the family. The remaining portion can be reinvested into the soil.

Additionally, as individuals learn to cultivate, they will develop a sense of responsibility that influences them to manage their finances wisely.

Your finance is too precious for you to waste any part of it.

Poultry

At their early stage of growth, much attention is needed, but thereafter, caring for poultry becomes less demanding. Once enough feed, water and light are given to them, they can be left unsupervised whilst you attend to work, school, shopping or rest. However, do not leave them unsupervised for very long periods.

The manure from the poultry can be used as organic nutrients for your plants, hence producing organic or healthier choices of food. The initial cash outlay for building the pen, buying water and feeding trays, and installing lighting will not have to be repeated on a regular basis.

Mammals

The rearing of mammals could be for reproduction, supplying meat or their by-products to markets, or the family's own consumption.

If you are patient enough, two animals will reproduce many of their kind. You will be required to provide enough food, water and proper shelter so that the animals will thrive and reproduce.

22. Preserve Your Valuable Antiques

Do not allow others to damage things in your possession that you would have loved to own for years. Persons who are smoking cigarettes should be kept far away from items such as your mattress, curtains or chairs since the fire from the cigarette can damage them. Your friends and family members must respect you and your possessions.

You cannot allow persons to borrow and return your possession in a damaged state. Let them repay or repair the damaged item. It may be hard to take these measures, but they are necessary to avoid a repeat event of having to replace your damaged items due to the inconsideration of others. Your hard-earned money is precious. What you purchase should not have a shortened life because of another person's misuse or abuse.

When your children are young and learning to move around, breakable items should be out of their reach. Do not allow your children to break all the things in the home. If you do, all you will be left with is a vehicle without wheels or a chair without legs.

Everything you pay for must be treated as a valuable investment. If you purchase some items for a particular season, store them once the season is over to be used again in future, so as to minimize waste.

Read the label or instructions, or ask questions concerning electrical items to ensure that you use the correct voltage on any of those appliances.

Do not allow food to boil over onto your stove or the refrigerator to become dirty. This will only reduce the life of the appliance and send you to the store again to purchase the same item, most likely at a higher price.

Stop leaks immediately to prevent the unnecessary expense of replacing materials, as in the case of wood or carpet or other household appliances. Purchase quality items that may cost a little more, rather than replacing items of inferior quality regularly, so as to save yourself a few dollars.

23. Secondhand Purchases

If you are purchasing a secondhand item, ensure that you are getting quality for your money and that you will be satisfied for a long time to come. Do not purchase secondhand items because the cost is low.

Secondhand purchases ought to be based on quality. Many times, you may end up spending much more when you purchase secondhand items. *It may seem that you purchased "the dead" and now need to purchase the casket.*

As the repair cost of secondhand items can be continuous and high, it is advisable that instead of purchasing what you are uncertain of, you go through the normal procedure and purchase a new item. New items ought to be purchased with warranty.

Ensure receipts or other forms of documentation are provided when you make a purchase. If the secondhand offer looks good but you are fearful about making the wrong decision, bring along an experienced person with you to clear any doubts.

Ask many questions, even if you think they are irrelevant, and you may be able to receive appropriate answers before a purchase is made. Once you are satisfied with the answers, go ahead and seal the deal.

Do not allow your fingers to be bitten thrice by repeating a bad choice. Do not purchase a secondhand item just because you feel indebted to the person making the offer.

24. Repairs and Maintenance

A house that is built to last for several years must be repaired and maintained. Vehicles of the best quality need regular repairs and maintenance. The absence of repairs and maintenance reduces the lifespan of things.

When items are not regularly repaired or maintained, you may have to replace them altogether sooner or bear higher repair costs. Failing to repair or replace a part of a motor vehicle may result in the complete replacement of other parts.

For example, the wheel of a vehicle needs to be realigned and greased, especially if the vehicle is driven on rough surface regularly. The engine oil for the machine needs to be changed and not allowed to accumulate. Check the machine for water, fuel, oil and air daily. Build a shed or garage for your vehicle or cover it with a cloth when you are not using it regularly.

Computers will need new virus scanning updates to combat new viruses. Similarly, a dentist will often advise persons to brush and clean their teeth regularly, as it may save them the expense of having to replace, remove, refill or recap their teeth.

25. Electricity and Electrical Appliances

When shopping for electrical appliances, take special care in choosing the brand; *take note of the manufacturing date, voltage, wattage, autoregulation (110V–220V), AC-DC changeover, etc.* Make sure to only purchase electrical appliances that come with a warranty.

Some electrical appliances are for household use and cannot be used for any additional purpose. If the voltage fluctuates regularly, then use a power strip, transformer, voltage regulator or uninterruptible power supply (UPS) as is necessary. With constant changes in voltage, electrical appliances will be damaged and soon you will have to replace them.

Purchase appliances with 50/60Hz. Electrical appliances should not be purchased or installed because they are less expensive. The wattage of some electrical appliances may be very high and will result in a high electricity bill. It is becoming more important to use environmentally friendly electrical appliances, including bulbs, fridges and microwave ovens.

Follow these additional simple tips to reduce electricity consumption:

- Do not overload your electrical circuits. Avoid using all your electrical appliances at once. Press your clothes when less electrical appliances are in use.

- Turn off or disconnect electrical appliances immediately after use. Gather all your clothes and then plug in the iron to press. After you have finished using the iron, disconnect it.

- Before you leave the house, check the house and ensure that all electrical appliances are turned off.

- Turn off electrical appliances, especially during thunderstorms, as they can damage your appliances. Ensure that your wiring system is earthed.

- Make sure to only purchase electrical appliances that come with a warranty.

- During holiday seasons, avoid using all lights at the same time. You can interchange different sets of lights to get the effect you are looking for.
- *Turn off the television, lights and other appliances when no one is using them.*

26. Reducing Unprofitable Expenses

Have you ever regretted going to a place or attending an occasion? Who will you blame? To make good sacrifices, you will have to say "No" to some people and "No" to some places as well.

Different occasions *may* require different styles of clothing, fancy hairstyles, transportation fees, entrance fees, etc., and most of the time, you will have to incur most of the expenses.

When purchasing clothes, resist purchasing clothes to wear just for one occasion. Choose clothes that may be used on several other occasions.

Grocery/Household Items

Do you visit the shop every time you have to prepare a meal? If possible, purchase wholesale quantities and perhaps receive discounts for them. Avoid purchasing small quantities, if you can afford to. When you purchase large quantities, you can share with someone else or reduce your regular visits to the supermarket. This can reduce excess spending.

Avoid cooking more than you are able to consume. The excess, if not shared with others or stored in the refrigerator, will be wasted. Avoid placing on your plate more food than you can consume.

How many pairs of shoes or articles of clothing do you have, *and how many do you really need?* Carefully and honestly consider this question and make appropriate choices.

Transportation

Sometimes, you can walk to your destination if the distance is short and you are not running late. Walking is a good form of exercise and will keep your body healthy and in shape. Your precious clothes may even fit you again. Some physical illnesses may also improve when you start to exercise.

Organize yourself so you are always ahead of time and not in a rush to complete things. Hurrying to do things may result in making mistakes or you having to rely on taxis if you do not have your own vehicle, despite your destination being within reasonable walking distance.

27. Security of Your Property and Possessions

Do not allow burglars to have you spending your money continually. Secure your building from vandals by placing grills or sensing devices. It will cost you now, but you will be able to better enjoy your hard-earned dollars in the long run.

Fence the yard, if necessary, as this is likely to keep unwanted guests off your properties, allowing you to sleep in peace at night. When the yard is unfenced, animals may destroy your clothes and feast on your kitchen garden. With a fenced yard, you can leave some of your possessions outside without the fear of anyone removing them.

Many times, because of unfenced yards or no other form of security, strangers can easily walk through your yard and remove valuables such as shoes, clothes, bicycles, garden tools, household appliances or garden plants.

Think about it: when you purchase an item on a hire purchase agreement, you will have to continually pay for it even when the item is no longer in your possession because of vandals.

28. Dispose of Damaged or Unnecessary Equipment/Items

How many cars, microwave ovens, washing machines, televisions, etc. do you need? There are some things that belong to you that *you will not use again.* If it is in *good condition,* you can sell it for a reasonable price or give it away.

There is no need for you to surround yourself with irreparable things that you no longer need. Broken teacups, saucers, pots, fans, irons and buckets are all dangerous to have around the house and may soon cost you. These damaged items can become homes to insects, etc. Dispose of them and enjoy the space within your dwelling area.

29. Choose Carefully When Purchasing from Individuals

Sometimes, hucksters or vendors will approach you to get you to purchase from them. They come with enticing or polished words that are soothing to the ear. Nevertheless, the prices that they charge you are much higher than what you will pay at a shop or supermarket.

As their customer, you may be paying for the time taken and distance covered for them to get to you. Sometimes, they may use an altered measuring instrument to weigh the item, so you end up paying more than the item is worth.

Think carefully when presented with a seemingly good deal. An item may be cheap and sweet, but the cost later may be greater. Cheapness may sometimes result in a higher price tag in the long run.

All these negative factors must not be associated with every vendor, but be alert when shopping to ensure that you receive value for money. Whatever you agree to pay for is what must be received.

It is difficult, if not impossible, to successfully prosecute dishonest vendors and hucksters, because they change location regularly. To top it off, what you will receive as a settlement from a person whose income is not fixed, is a big question.

30. Use Professionals to Perform Professional Work

Learning to do many things is very important, but you may not be skilled enough to do everything yourself. Do not try to run a marathon when you are best at sprinting short distances. Do what you know best and leave the rest to those who can provide a professional service or advice.

Avoid damaging things in the house, especially household appliances, by trying to fix them without the necessary skills. It will cost you more than hiring a professional to do the job.

Hire a professional you feel comfortable dealing with and in whom you have confidence to meet your needs. After dealing with the professional, you should have enough energy left to smile, laugh and share your testimony rather than wasting time and money, without achieving the right result.

Try to find professionals who are established. Some professionals are more concerned about how much extra money they can charge you rather than providing a professional service. Look out for such individuals and avoid them.

If your needs are properly addressed by those whom you have utilized, try to keep them around, especially if their prices and services are acceptable to you and your family. Some professionals are good to retain as they know your history, your business, your family (e.g., the family doctor, mechanic, carpenter, driver, etc.). Employing the service of a professional who is not familiar with you may ultimately cost you more, as he or she may take some time to understand and properly address your needs.

31. During the Holidays

Many holidays have a specific meaning or reason. However, some people misunderstand and abuse a holiday and see it as a time for much eating and drinking. Many persons have spent large and wasteful sums of money during such a time. Sometimes, the money spent is borrowed and would have to be repaid with interest or repaid out of one's savings account. Once the holiday season is over, it is time for repayment to begin.

Many persons like to cook in excess of what the family can consume. Some of the food from the large quantity cooked goes wasted. Instead of allowing excess food and other items go to waste, give them to charitable institutions and needy individuals.

You may not need to repaint the house that was recently painted. Count the cost of all the things that you do for the holiday season and see if they are really needed. Review your purchases to see if they were all necessary.

If you feel that you want to be merry and share your feelings with others, be careful of your spending. Remember that in whatever month you choose to celebrate the holiday, your income remains the same, unless you are entitled to fringe benefits.

The stress and pressure that some persons cause are unnecessary. Remember the holiday is not about wasteful feasting, but fun and fellowship. However, efforts must be made to remember the main reason for the season. Think about the approaching new year and identify some of the areas in which you can reduce expenditure.

If the house that you are living in needs a renovation, consider having it done now instead of waiting till when the cost of certain materials increases.

Monitor your utility bills (electricity, phone, water, gas, etc.) within this period to keep those expenditures at a manageable amount.

32. Transportation Services

If your business is to offer transportation services, remember to provide a quality and efficient service to all your customers, for it will speak volumes about you and your business.

If making money is your primary focus, then soon you may damage your vehicle, cause harm to others and fail to realize your expectations. The driver and the vehicle may become liabilities to the owner if they are involved in an accident.

Overloading is a dangerous practice and an offence that will cause you more than you earn. There is a high price for overloading, dangerous driving and violating traffic laws. Insurance companies may disqualify you if your vehicle gets into an accident, because of the breaching of insurance and road (traffic) regulations.

All vehicles are built to maneuver comfortably while carrying weight within a specified range. Overloading will add to repair and maintenance costs quickly and continuously. Overloaded and overworked vehicles will break down sooner or later, so exercise care at all times. Like humans, machines need rest too.

Law enforcers are out there to enforce the law and anyone found violating the law would be given the relevant penalties. Sometimes, overloading the vehicle will cause the driver and vehicle to be detained at the police station. Time and finances wasted while being detained are time and finances lost to the owner, especially if the vehicle is your source income.

Owners, ensure that your vehicle is used for the purpose(s) specified. The vehicle is meant to perform according to the manufacturer's specifications.

Make your vehicle attractive to the public. It should have a refreshing scent and be clean always. In the case of a taxi, you can check your backseat after dropping your passengers to ensure that it has been left clean enough for your next customer. With a van or truck, you can use well-advertised labels, such as telephone numbers and descriptions of the services provided.

Maintenance of your vehicles is quite important. Arrange for timely checkup and servicing.

33. Household Expenses

Household expenses should never be more than you can handle, because you may not be able to bail yourself out, and this will hurt you. Expenses should never be like a mountain, where you are unable to see over it. You must plan your expenses in such a way that you are able to have breathing space.

Many expenses may have you overextended, so that even if an opportunity comes your way you are unable to maximize it. This won't happen if you plan your expenditure early on.

Most expenses, if neglected within their specified time of payment, can cause you to pay more or affect your ability to take care of other expenditures. For example, failing to pay your electricity bills may cause you to pay more in the future, or you may have to pay a reconnection fee. If the expenses are more than you can handle, you may face embarrassment, lose friends and family, have to seek refinancing options or have services withheld or disconnected.

All expenses should fit within your income and still leave space for other opportunities that may arise. Your expenses should never be 100% of your income.

Telephone Bills

Avoid making your telephone bill higher than you can pay. Your telephone bill will be reduced if you reduce the length of your phone conservations.

If you have friends or relatives living abroad, use other means of communicating with them that are less expensive. If you have to mail a letter or card, allow ample time for delivery as mailing things at the last minute costs a lot more than regular post.

If you have to call someone who is overseas, call him or her early in the morning or in the evening. During these off-peak periods, the rate charged is much lower. Fortunately, with so many modern ways to communicate, telephone expenses have become lower now than in previous decades.

Before making a call, write down all that you want to say and have the information at hand. End the conversation once your message has been delivered. Avoid prolonging a conversation if the phone call is expensive.

As parents, regulate children's use of the telephone by possibly inserting a password or code, or using telephone cards.

The Internet has made communication much easier and cheaper. You just need to dial up or log on and start your conversation with the intended person. This means of communication is very low in cost and in some situations, free. With the Internet, you can also type your message, press send and wait for the reader to respond.

34. Follow Safety Regulations

Prevention is better than cure. If you would stop for just a minute and think about the consequences of doing something without any protection and increasing your risk of sustaining injuries, you may want to reconsider your actions.

All manufacturers think it best to include safety guidelines for their products, and persons who do not fully understand the danger should adhere to their suggestions. Just consider what would happen if you disobeyed the safety rules and hurt yourself, your family or the property that you occupy? Sometimes, one wrong action may cause a significant change in your family's life.

What about driving a vehicle without enough engine oil or with a damaged wheel? Eventually, the vehicle will be damaged or written off and you will have to bear the cost of replacing that vehicle.

It is advisable to place computers in a cool environment or in a place where there is adequate ventilation. Not heeding this instruction from the manufacturer will soon result in damage to the computer; hence a replacement would have to be made.

A simple hair-cutting machine that is not taken care of after use will soon also have to be replaced. Obeying simple instructions will save you money.

Some persons have tried to work on electrical equipment with exposed or damaged wires. This practice, if not professionally done, may cause damage to property or even loss of life in the case of an entire home being engulfed in fire.

Patience may be a good attribute to exercise sometimes. Wait until the traffic light has turned green before moving. Failing to adhere to this requirement will cost you. You may have to pay a heavy fine for breaching this traffic regulation.

Sometimes, breaching a traffic regulation may result in an accident, which means needing to send your vehicle as well as another person's for repair.

When this happens, either you or your insurance company will have to bear the cost.

Worse still, lives are sometimes lost because of one's impatience. How many traffic offences have you or someone you know had to pay for this year? Did it increase costs?

Reference List

CAT Interactive Text, Level C, Paper 5. 1998. *Managing Finances*. 1st edn. London: BPP Publishing. ISBN 0751700983

About the Author

You do not have to become an economist, a banker or a finance manager in order to manage your own finances. Follow some of the simple techniques that Geary Reid has shared, and your life can become better financially. Some of these techniques can be done within your home or place of employment. Many successful persons have followed these very techniques, and that is why they are experiencing success today.

The choices people make will affect the amount of funds available to them. Persons sometimes want to impress others, so they go out of their way to purchase items that they do not need, just as they eat foods that have a negative impact on their health. It is important not to be a people-pleaser, but to do the right thing and manage your finances so that you do not have to depend on others to provide you with handouts.

This page is intentionally left blank.

This page is intentionally left blank.

This page is intentionally left blank.

This page is intentionally left blank.

This page is intentionally left blank.

This page is intentionally left blank.

This page is intentionally left blank.

This page is intentionally left blank.

This page is intentionally left blank.

This page is intentionally left blank.

This page is intentionally left blank.

This page is intentionally left blank.